In The Reign Of The

KEIGHLEY AND DISTRICT IN EDWA ... S

Compiled by Ian De...

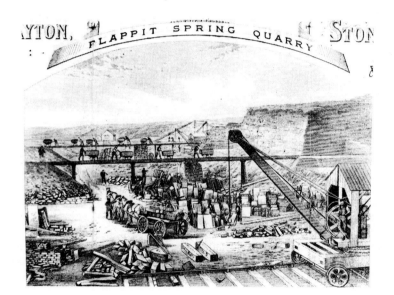

This busy engraving, enlarged from a billhead from Flappit Spring Quarry at Cullingworth, is a reminder of the local stone which supported a period of intense building development. Quarries were active on most of the surrounding hills.

The occupation was dangerous. At Flappit Spring Quarry in July, 1904, David Bravery died under four tons of falling earth; another two workmen narrowly managed to jump out of the way. Two days later Adam Pedley was seriously injured by the premature explosion of a charge whilst blasting at Haworth Moor Quarry.

Published by Hendon Publishing Co.Ltd., Hendon Mill, Nelson, Lancashire

Text © Ian Dewhirst, 1993

Printed by Turner and Earnshaw Ltd., Westway House, Sycamore Avenue, Burnley.

INTRODUCTION

Although King Edward VII came to the throne in 1901 and died in 1910, the tone of English life during a slightly wider period, from the turn of the century to the outbreak of the Great War, seems distinctively his, Edwardian.

Black-bordered local newspapers, commenting on his sudden death, called him Edward the Peacemaker. The *Keighley News* stressed his delight 'in the display not of kingliness but of kindliness, and he succeeded wherever he went in conveying an impression not so much of power as of peacefulness.' He became immediately a 'Sovereign of Happy Memory', and a similar sense of well-being and nostalgia quickly came to symbolise his times. Key points from the sermons preached locally in his memory, as headlined in the press, suggested the flavour of the late King and his reign: 'Goodwill and Peace' (Laycock); 'Peace and Humanitarianism' (Oxenhope); 'Greater Than a Warrior' (Silsden); 'A Wise and Sagacious Ruler' (Oakworth); 'A King for the People' (Ingrow); 'Not Only a King But a Man' (Steeton). As a local grocer had put it, on glimpsing the King at Doncaster Races in 1903: 'Homely looking old fellow is Ned'!

The Edwardian age was nationally comfortable and confident, and represented a high-water mark in the history of a place like Keighley. Its great mills were fully employed, and the town was palpably developing. Thoroughfares were widened, amenities were improved, whilst a relatively new Borough Council was enthusiastic and imbued with civic pride. Yet the fascination of the period lies largely in its contrasts, in the way life changed within a few years from the traditional to the modern. In 1900, trams and fire engines were still drawn by horses, cows and sheep stood for sale in the streets, some mills still used water-power and an occasional handloom weaver survived. But soon all that was to change.

A striking feature of the age was its flamboyance. Local Edwardians turned out in their thousands — sometimes in their tens of thousands — on any pretext. Royal occasions, galas, visiting religious leaders or circuses, elections, fires — all brought large numbers of people together. Some would even catch trains to go to watch a good fire!

This impression of life in and around Keighley in those days admits a bias towards the flamboyant, for photographers tended to record occasions rather than the everyday. Assuredly, there were many Edwardian photographers. The postcard was enjoying its heyday, with small local stationers producing their own, whilst an active Keighley and District Photographic Association had been in existence since 1889. Sadly, however, it is rarely possible to link an individual name with certainty to a specific picture.

The following photographs have been collected over four decades, and I am indebted to the many kind townsfolk who have lent or given me examples. Special thanks are due to the late David Collins and Stewart Owen of Howarth Photography, who have painstakingly brought out the 'latent image' in some creased and faded originals.

September, 1993.

Ian Dewhirst

This photograph, taken from an upper window of the Craven Bank in North Street on a raw day, February 2nd, 1901, shows some of the 20,000 people who, despite the weather, assembled to hear the Proclamation of King Edward VII, packing the centre of Keighley within approximate earshot of a platform in front of the Court House.

All eyes are directed to a small group of raised figures: the Mayor and Assistant Town Clerk, the Mace-Bearer in ceremonial robes and cocked hat, and two trumpeters of the 2nd West Yorkshire Artillery. Behind them, inside the railings, are magistrates and notabilities ('the flower of our local authorities,' according to the press).

A close examination of this photograph through a magnifying-glass suggests that it was possibly taken in a moment prior to the singing of the National Anthem, as a brass band at the foot the platform have their instruments to their lips, whilst a number of men are in the act of doffing their hats. Significantly, most of the men directly in front of the platform are bare-headed, many immediately behind are taking their hats off, whilst those to the right of the platform still have their heads covered; which shows that the crowd in front hears best whereas those at the sides are having difficulty in following what is going on!

This view of North Street probably dates from 1901, when the road had been widened but the lamps had not yet been set back along the left-hand side. In the distance, opposite the Mechanics' Institute clock-tower, a tree stands isolated where garden walls have been removed. At least two pedestrians still seem uncertain as to which is the road and which the pavement!

This part of Keighley had been substantially rebuilt during the 1890s. Three men on the left are about to enter the Star Hotel, which had superseded 'a little old-fashioned white-washed place' and had sold more ale than ever during its rebuilding. Beyond, a space waits to be filled in.

The theatrical-looking gentleman in the foreground is Tom Waddington, a local entertainer who used to organise 'Monster Christmas Carnivals' at the Temperance Hall, billed as 'refined and suitable for all'.

Turn-of-the-century Lawkholme was one of a number of separate hamlets on the verge of being absorbed into Keighley proper. When this photograph was taken, Lawkholme was still semi-rural, a few houses and farm buildings at the corner of Lawkholme Lane and the present Hard Ings Road.

Here Lawkholme Lane runs from the right across the middle of the view — beyond the field where what appears to be cricket is being played — to continue at right-angles to join Bradford Road. The abundant trees of Eastwood House or Victoria Park dominate the right-hand background.

The development of Lawkholme as a residential suburb had been recognised in 1898 by the opening of a Lawkholme Co-operative Store, and the fields shown here would soon be built over.

On the other hand, some Edwardian communities were subsequently to diminish or change beyond recognition. This is Thwaites, clustered precisely at the foot of Thwaites Brow Road, which used to hold its own annual gala. Virtually all the buildings on the left half of this photograph have since disappeared.

Road traffic from Keighley to Bradford and Leeds still crossed the River Aire at Stockbridge by this rural bridge, built in 1671 and widened in 1754 — and indeed would continue to do so till 1929.

This beautiful photograph was probably taken by Taylor Smith, agent for the Horsfall family's Hayfield and Malsis estates and a man "of a quiet and unassuming disposition". Apparently a prolific amateur photographer whose work has never enjoyed recognition, he seems to have had a flair for recording crowd scenes from upper windows, and a number of the more spectacular photographs in this book may well be his.

A number of Keighley public-houses were rebuilt on a grander scale around the turn of the century. This is the original Albert Hotel in Bridge Street, set back behind rockery gardens.

In September of 1899, Keighley Corporation approved plans submitted by Timothy Taylor and Co., of the Knowle Spring Brewery, for a new Albert Hotel intended as 'an improvement to the town'. This featured two smoke rooms, filling bar, vault, bar parlour, club room and, in deference to the business transacted in hostelries, a commercial room.

A little of the new Albert Hotel appears on the far left of this view of the corner of Bridge Street and Church Street. The kind of shops shown here — away from the newly-developed principal thoroughfares — had changed little during the past half-century and more. J. Crabtree's Boot and Shoe Warehouse still sports an old-fashioned trade sign shaped like a long curly shoe, whilst the shop-front of hosier Thomas Hobson looks Dickensian.

On May 18th, 1901, some 20,000 townspeople turned out in Keighley to give 'a joyful and enthusiastic welcome home' to 27 citizen soldiers of the First Active Service Contingent of the 3rd Volunteer Battalion of the Duke of Wellington's West Riding Regiment, who had left for the Boer War in South Africa sixteen months before.

Here, led by Captain Edgar Dewhurst of Skipton, escorted by the rest of the Battalion and distinguishable by their khaki uniforms and khaki-covered helmets, the men of the Active Service Contingent march from the railway station along East Parade into Low Street on their way to a Thanksgiving Service at Keighley Parish Church, where the Rector, the Revd. H. J. Palmer, delivered an address of welcome. This was followed by more speeches at the Drill Hall, and a banquet four days later in the Mechanics' Institute.

Local Ambulance Volunteers and Imperial Yeomanry had also been eager to get to South Africa, whilst by late 1901 a Keighley and District Patriotic Fund — formed to assist the wounded and the dependents of servicemen — had raised £4,438-10s.-11d.

During the afternoon of Coronation Day, a procession of some thirty historical tableaux arranged by local Sunday Schools paraded through Keighley, where an estimated 30,000 spectators lined the streets, including 12,000 Sunday School children in North Street who sang 'God Save the King'.

The tableaux depicted such highlights of English history as 'The Signing of Magna Carta' and 'The Game of Bowls on Plymouth Hoe', even the recent Peace at Pretoria which had ended the Boer War. Prizes went to St Mary's Church School's 'Edward III Releasing the Burghers of Calais' and Upper Green Congregational School's 'The Sailing of the Mayflower'.

This photograph shows 'Pope Gregory and the Saxon Children' — the offering of St Barnabas's Church at Thwaites Brow — moving off along East Parade from the Great Northern Railway goods yard where the procession was marshalled. In a few minutes it will begin to drizzle!

At Keighley, Coronation Day in 1902 also witnessed a memorial stone-laying for the Carnegie Free Library. Keighley's was, indeed, the first library in England substantially paid for by the Scots-born American industrialist Andrew Carnegie. This informal snapshot shows dignitaries taking advantage of the raised library site — protected by mundane hoardings covered with posters — to watch, presumably, the historical tableaux procession in North Street over the heads of the crowd.

The bare-headed man in front of the further flag is Sir Swire Smith, the Keighley mill-owner whose educational interests and friendship with Andrew Carnegie had made him the ideal performer of the stone-laying ceremony. Presented with a silver trowel and oak mallet, he had, according to the local press, 'spread the mortar, and laid the memorial stone in a workmanlike manner'. In his speech he had related the conversation leading to Carnegie's generosity towards Keighley:

'Mr. Carnegie said 'What is your population?' I replied about 42,000. 'Why,' said he, '£10,000 would build you a library' to which I replied, 'Yes it would.' Without more ado he said, 'Well, I will give you a library.'

The Stars and Stripes seen flying in the foreground is in honour of Andrew Carnegie, who was unable to be present.

Bonfires and illuminations brightened the dusk of Coronation Day, 1902. Upwards of 30,000 visited Victoria Park to see the Mansion House and lawns lit 'on a scale of dazzling splendour' by 1,177 gas lamps and 5,133 candle buckets, so that the building seemed 'luminous from top to bottom, lines of living coloured fire scoring its facade in all directions'. The weary man seen here sitting on his ladders looks as if he has just put most of those lights in place!

The elaborate porch on the left formed the entrance to Keighley's museum, which had opened in 1899 and proceeded to accumulate a varied collection, largely through donations. Colonel Sugden of Oakworth gave a 'stuffed crocodile from the River Nile', Herbert Smith the skull of a hippopotamus, whilst Isaac Bailey's 'gift of curiosities' included South African assegais and relics of Waterloo and the Franco-Prussian War. There was quite a run of 'stones from inside of horses'. When Messrs Rowntree and Co. Ltd. offered '14 samples of cocoa with leaves and pods of cocoa trees', the Mayor was deputed to ensure that these did not 'take the form of an advertisement'.

By 1904, Keighley was commended for its museum 'such as few Yorkshire towns can boast'.

Oakworth House, a mid-Victorian mansion 'in the Italian style', was built by woolcombing magnate Sir Isaac Holden as the Worth Valley's 'principal attraction'.

Born in Scotland in 1807, son of a small farmer and lead miner, Holden had worked from an early age, eventually becoming book-keeper, then manager, then partner at Townend Brothers of Cullingworth. 'I stayed with them twelve months,' he would characteristically reminisce about when he gave notice to leave the firm, 'and during that time trained three young men to take my place.' Later head of a great combing concern in Bradford and France, Holden lived on a staple diet of fruit, would walk from Oakworth to his Bradford works, and rode his pony on his ninetieth birthday.

Oakworth House took ten years to build, its grounds complete with grottoes, orangeries, orchid houses, vineries, a Turkish bath-house, and a winter garden covering half an acre. French workmen built rockeries, Italian craftsmen laid mosaic floors. Even the adjoining Oakworth Methodist Chapel — seen here on the right — which had been 'liberally subscribed for' by Sir Isaac, acted as 'an ornamental and useful appendage'. Distinguished visitors included Andrew Carnegie, John Bright, Lord Rosebery and the Duke of Devonshire.

Following Sir Isaac's death in 1897, however, the house, despite having been offered for sale by auction, stood empty for a number of years, some of its rooms dismantled. One winter Saturday in 1909, a joiner lit a fire in the library, and early next morning the premises were found well alight. Keighley Fire Brigade refused to attend, since Oakworth did not subscribe to its funds, and the Oakworth brigade was left to a hopeless struggle using inadequate appliances.

In 1925 the grounds of Oakworth House became the village's public park. Only the portico of the mansion itself remains.

An experiment in what would now be called town-twinning began at Whitsuntide in 1905 when, under the auspices of the Keighley Chamber of Commerce and the Trades and Labour Council, 32 local workmen were sent on a visit to the Parisian suburb of Suresnes. That September a similar number of French workmen came to Keighley.

Their visit roused enormous interest. Their arriving train was heralded by detonating fog-signals, and they were met by their Keighley counterparts wearing button-holes of red, white and blue sweet-peas 'arranged in the form of the tricolour', both visitors and hosts passing 'through lines of interested spectators' to tea at the Mansion House in Victoria Park.

The Frenchmen spent a week being shown the sights of the neighbourhood. On being conducted round Lund Park they exclaimed 'Magnifique!' and 'Grande!' in appreciation of the views, whilst at Messrs Bottomley's sweet factory they watched special 'L'Entente Cordiale' rock being made in their honour.

Here both French and local parties pose for a group photograph on a visit to Cliffe Castle. In the centre at the front, with his hat on his knee, sits Henry Isaac Butterfield, its owner and builder. A cosmopolitan worsted magnate with French and American connections, he was able to address his foreign visitors in their own language, and he personally showed them round his mid-Victorian 'castle'.

This frame from a fragment of early cinematograph film shows bystanders waiting for some unidentified street event in Keighley. It is interesting for its unselfconscious line-up of a cross-section of people. The well-dressed lady in the large hat towards the right-hand side contrasts vividly with the group of women on the left, three of whom are clutching their voluminous shawls under their chins. At least two boys near the bicycle are wearing clogs. The cloth-capped man on the right of the lady in the hat has just lit a cigarette, whilst the second and third women from the left are holding their babies. The elegant little boy on the left of the man in the straw hat contrasts with the grubby-looking smaller child dimly visible next to the woman in black at the far left. In the yard of each house is a post on which to hang washing-lines.

Touring spectacles were not uncommon. Barnum and Bailey's Greatest Show on Earth visited Keighley in 1899, arriving in four special trains totalling seventy railway cars, and parading the streets with cages of lions, tigers and leopards, panthers, hyenas, bears and wolves, and a chariot drawn by zebras. Buffalo Bill Cody's Wild West Show came in 1903, complete with 800 people, 500 horses, and covered stands to accommodate 14,000 spectators.

This photograph probably shows the elephants and camels of Sanger's Circus parading through the drizzle along North Street in March, 1902. The jumbled area beyond the hoardings — site of a future Town Hall Square — is the Corporation stone-yard; in the background is Cavendish Street with the Mechanics' Institute and the United Methodist Free Church.

At the time there was a smallpox epidemic in the North of England, and Keighley's Medical Officer of Health visited Sanger's Circus at Colne the day before it was due in Keighley, to inspect all its employees — luckily none showed signs of smallpox, nor had the circus performed at any infected towns.

Nothing better conveys the sense of excitement which such shows brought into workaday communities than a little girl's school composition about her visit to 'Bostock and Wombwell's No. 1 Menagerie' in 1910. 'Captain Wombwell went into a den of lions and performed many amusing tricks,' she wrote. 'He made the lions jump different heights. Then he opened the lion's mouth and put his head inside its jaws.'

There were camels and dromedaries, 'placid creatures who looked at you through their small eyes and munch the biscuits and the nuts which are given to them by the boys and girls'; a porcupine, a wolf, a bison, a wild boar ('a black pig with tusks to defend itself'), an emu, a mandrill and a cage-full of smaller monkeys; lions and tigers 'and one animal which was half a lion and half a tiger which when at first bought cost ninety guineas and is now laid dying'.

PROSPECT MILL FROM THE EAST.

An example of the great factory complexes which characterised the urban landscape, Prospect Mill at Ingrow was one of four operated by Messrs Wright Brothers, worsted spinners and manufacturers — their other three were Lumbfoot, Damems and Ingrams Mills. As so often the case, there was a connection between mill and place of worship, James Wright being a Trustee both of Wesley Place and Hermit Hole Wesleyan Methodist Chapels. All four mills closed for the day of his funeral in 1913.

An electric tram can be seen here in the left background in Halifax Road.

VIEW FROM LEEMING OXENHOPE.

Far from being rural villages, Worth Valley communities by the early century were enjoying an industrial heyday. Viewed here from the direction of Leeming, Oxenhope appears dominated by the smoky chimneys of its worsted premises, Holme and Perseverance Mills and Lowertown Shed.

Oxenhope was notably self-sufficient. Its stone merchants supplied the wherewithal for its sturdy terraces and villas; coal and lime merchants were represented at its station yard. Oxenhope even boasted two co-operative societies.

Little old Worth Valley factories still prospered, like Dunkirk Mill, a busy concern surrounded by fields, cows and hens. Here Joseph Dewhirst, spindle band maker, rope and twine manufacturer, corn miller and commission wool comber, was also synonymous with Marsh Wesleyan Chapel, where he served as class leader, treasurer, Sunday School superintendent and secretary of the Band of Hope.

When his two daughters became engaged, he built them the twin houses seen in the right background. They married on the same day, both at Lowertown Wesleyan Methodist Chapel, dressed alike, returning to identical homes furnished the same, except that one of them had a piano as the bridegroom was musical!

Despite the proliferation of factories, cottage industries survived here and there into the twentieth century. The last handloom weaver in the Worth Valley was Timmy Feather, seen here with his bobbin-winder outside his cottage at Buckley Green, Stanbury. He would die in 1910 at the age of 85.

Indeed, Timmy Feather's life-style was older than the Industrial Revolution. A bachelor, porridge formed his staple diet. His loom shared his upstairs room with his bed and tubs of meal, whilst his downstairs kitchen was described as an 'old curiosity shop' crammed with chests, pots, empty bird-cages, treacle-tins, cases of stuffed birds, clocks... He kept hens, which were in the habit of walking indoors. Over the decades he is estimated to have woven 234,780 yards of cotton cloth, pressing the treadles of his loom 540 million times!

In his later years, recognised as the last of his type, he became virtually an object of pilgrimage for writers, photographers and school classes.

One of the original recipients of an old age pension, Timmy greeted it with Pennine drollery. 'Well! Aw niver knew nought like it!' he exclaimed. 'They browt a looad o' coils afoor Kursmiss, an' now five shillin' i' t'week as long as aw live! An' aw've done nowt for nawther on 'em!'

Water remained a viable source of power into the present century, as witness this waterwheel at Bridgehouse Mills, Haworth.

Order-books of Keighley foundry engineers E. A. Roper and Co. Ltd. record that in July of 1904 the Bridgehouse Mill Company requested 36 new waterwheel buckets, each 8 feet 10⅞ inches long. Fixing these in position required 20 dozen side bolts, 13 dozen stay bolts, 42 dozen new bolts and six dozen wood battens in red deal. Late the following year a further urgent order — 'per telephone' — required another 'Dozen Water Wheel Buckets to be fixed on Saturdays, as early as convenient'.

E. A. Roper and Co. subsequently added a note to the order: 'Since these were supplied it has been found that if they had been ¼ inch shorter it would have saved time in fixing. In future let the length be 8 ft. 10⅝ ins.'

The condition of the buckets shown here suggests that the photograph was taken prior to July, 1904.

Other waterwheels used into the twentieth century were at Damems Mill and Oakworth Corn Mill.

FIRE AT BOCKING MILL JULY 11th 1911

This photograph of a fire at Bocking Mill in 1911 — one of several enterprising local postcards to feature the event — serves as a reminder of the industrial hazards of warm summers.

In 1911 Bocking Mill was occupied by worsted manufacturers Ernest H. Gates and Co.. Early in the sunny evening of July 11th, shortly after most of their 200 employees had left for the day, smoke was spotted coming from the upper part of the four-storey warehouse. Within a couple of hours the building had been gutted, despite the efforts of four fire brigades. Fortunately, iron doors prevented the flames from spreading to the rest of the premises.

The fire was thought to have been caused by 'the concentration of the sun's rays through the heavy glass windows', inside which 'everything must have been as dry as matchwood'. Several thousands turned out to watch what the *Keighley News* of the time described as 'a fine spectacle from the neighbouring hill-sides'.

The Bocking Mill fire demonstrated how local mill-owners supported one another. Messrs Merrall sent their own works fire brigade to reinforce those from Haworth, Keighley and Bingley, whilst the Grove Mills traction waggon hauled the Keighley Brigade's heavy steam fire engine from Ingrow, as 'the horses at the end of a hot day's work had great difficulty in dragging it up the road'. For good measure, Boy Scouts marched up from Ingrow and Wesley Place to help the police keep back the crowds.

AIREDALE MILL FIRE. MARCH 31. 1906.
GW.

One of the more serious fires of the era, which destroyed a local landmark, was at Airedale Mill, beside the main Keighley to Skipton road at Kildwick, on March 31st, 1906. The two lower floors were occupied by Messrs T. Aked and Sons, spinners and manufacturers of genappe — a worsted yarn used for braids — and the third storey and garret by S. D. Watson, a worsted spinner who lived in an adjoining house.

The fire started on the second floor and probably spread via driving ropes. First spotted at 10 o'clock on a Saturday night, the whole mill was ablaze by the time the Skipton and Keighley fire brigades arrived.

Hundreds of sightseers congregated, a few travelling by motor-car and many by train from Keighley and Skipton. The local press waxed into purple prose in describing 'something grand and gloriously exciting in the lurid glow, the millions of shooting sparks, the palpitating of the three fire engines, and the countryside bathed in blood-red light'. At the height of the inferno, the flames rose above the mill chimney seen here.

An especially sad feature of this fire concerned the home of Mr and Mrs Watson, who had only recently been married. Their house was in fact saved but, under the impression that it would be burned, over-enthusiastic helpers had broken in and removed the furniture, damaging it in the process. Additionally, amid the confusion, the rooms were systematically vandalised and looted.

In conjuction with a destructive fire at Farnhill Mill the previous December, the Airedale Mill fire had the effect of throwing most of the population of Kildwick and Farnhill out of work.

After eighty years of relying on horses — including, for a number of years prior to 1904, some borrowed from the horse-trams! — Keighley Corporation Fire Brigade took a first step into the motor age in 1909 with the acquisition of an Argyll petrol fire tender.

Of fifty horse-power, equipped with 'the latest type of chemical extinguisher' and a sixty-foot telescope fire escape letting down on to its own wheels, this could accommodate six firemen. It was duly christened *Best* after Alderman John Best, chairman of the Fire Brigade Committee.

In 1910 Keighley Corporation acquired a second motor fire engine made by Dennis Brothers Ltd. of Guildford. With a sixty horse-power engine, this carried 'a turbine pump capable of delivering 450 gallons of water per minute at a pressure of 140 lbs.', storage for 600 yards of hose-pipe, 36 feet of extension ladders, room for ten firemen and a top speed of 40 miles per hour, even up 'any of the hills in Keighley'. The tyres on what were still being quaintly termed its 'hind' wheels were eleven inches broad compared with those of seven inches on its front wheels, 'so that if the motor has to be taken into a soft field it will be less liable to sink'.

During a twelve-month period in 1910-1911, Keighley Fire Brigade was called to some thirty fires, many in industrial premises.

The low-lying fields of the Aire Valley have always been liable to flooding. This scene near Utley was probably recorded in November of 1901, when a lengthy spell of dry weather was followed by a series of showers increasing to 'a steady and continuous rain' for two days.

Three inches of rain were registered in 48 hours; the Rivers Aire and Worth and the North Beck overflowed their banks; and a sheet of water submerged thousands of acres between Gargrave and Saltaire.

On the whole, however, Airedale suffered much less damage and disruption than neighbouring, narrower Calderdale.

This atmospheric scene demonstrates the effect of snow. It is five minutes past two in the afternoon in the centre of Keighley, yet nothing stirs except a milk float. The Mechanics' Institute, which housed the Municipal Hall, the School of Science and Art and the Trade and Grammar School, was Keighley's most prestigious building, and its clock-tower marked the focal-point of the town. On the right, a Town Hall Square bordered by shrubs has replaced the Corporation stone-yard shown in several other photographs.

In an era of enthusiastic church and chapel-going, congregations did not always worship in great buildings and the colloquial 'tin' mission was not uncommon. St Peter's, Halifax Road, started in an iron structure, St Barnabas's at Thwaites Brow and the Primitive Methodists of South Street in wooden ones.

This iron mission served St James's at Cross Roads from 1887 till 1909. Even such a temporary building cost £450. Here were held morning and evening services, with Holy Communion on the second and fourth Sundays each month. There was a 'very well attended' Sunday School in separate premises.

The last services were held here on August 29th, 1909, immediately before work began on a new St James's Parish Church on the same site, to be consecrated by the Bishop of Ripon in 1910. In the meantime, the congregation worshipped in their Sunday School.

For years from 1910, Oakworth held an annual Nonconformist Sunday School Festival each July. Slack Lane Baptists, Lane Ends Primitive Methodists, and Bogthorn and Oakworth Wesleyans would walk in procession through streets decorated with flags and bunting. Hymns were sung and addresses given, and sometimes wildflower bouquets would be judged.

Here, immaculate in their best clothes, worshippers listen to an address outside the gates of Oakworth Methodist Chapel. Some are holding their hymn-sheets, which included both words and music and sold at a penny each. It is poignant to realise that this may be the fifth such Festival, on July 11th, 1914 — if so, the Great War is less than a month away. The final hymn on the 1914 sheets was entitled 'The Call to Action'.

In 1905 General William Booth of the Salvation Army made a 'great northward motor-car tour', including a weekend at Keighley in his itinerary. On Saturday morning, August 12th, six motor-cars bearing the General and his staff drove into town, where crowds were waiting to cheer him despite his being late through having stopped to give an impromptu address to the inmates of the Halifax Workhouse Hospital.

Here the General stands up in his motor-car as it passes St Peter's Church in Halifax Road, exactly as the *Keighley Herald* had described him — a 'bare-headed veteran, clad in a long green coat, and with the wind playing in his long snowy locks and flowing beard'.

For the next two days Keighley was involved in Salvation Army activities, the "familiar 'Blood and Fire' uniform" being met with everywhere. The General was accorded a civic reception at the Municipal Hall, and the Queen's Theatre was placed at his disposal for two 'densely crowded' meetings. On Sunday evening he preached to 2,500, whilst an overflow of another 1,500 listened outside to Commissioner Cadman and Major Gregory, known as 'Red Hot Tom'. There were fifty converts.

Mr John Brigg of Kildwick Hall, Keighley's Member of Parliament since 1895, visits his Central Liberal Committee Rooms in the new Liberal Club Buildings in Scott Street at the time of the 1900 General Election.

His election leaflets, listing measures he had hitherto supported, provide an idea of the man: the Sale of Intoxicating Liquor to Children Bill, the extension of Sunday closing in Wales, reduction of hours in shops, workmen's cheap trains... Magistrate, worsted manufacturer, deacon of Devonshire Street Congregational Chapel, traveller, amateur geologist, he was in 1900 an active 66-year-old despite having had his right leg amputated the previous year.

This election was noteworthy for the way rosettes, medallions and party emblems were worn 'to an extent never previously seen in Keighley', and on polling day both Mr Brigg and his Conservative adversary were each given the use of a motor-car. Mr Brigg was re-elected by a majority of 640; nor would this be his last General Election. He would be knighted in 1909 and would die in harness two years later.

Mrs W. C. Anderson, wife of Keighley's Labour candidate at a Parliamentary Bye-election in 1911, canvasses children and a small dog!

Sir John Brigg, Liberal M.P. for the Keighley Division since 1895, had died that September. The resulting bye-election was described as short, 'keen and interesting' — it was all over within a month.

By tradition Keighley was a Liberal town, but on this occasion the Liberal candidate was challenged by both Conservative and Labour. The intensity of interest aroused was demonstrated by a public debate in the Skating Rink, attended by an astonishing 8,000, between Liberal Stanley O. Buckmaster, K.C., and Labour's William C. Anderson. They made a contrasting pair. Buckmaster had taken silk in 1902; Anderson, with his 'good Scottish day-school education' supplemented by evening classes, was an organiser for shop workers and chairman of the National Independent Labour Party.

The King's Council found himself up against the 'popular platform appeal' of an experienced trade unionist with a voice of 'remarkable carrying power', and the meeting broke up in disorder. 'Irresponsible youths' and many 'rather excitable persons of every shade of political opinion' were blamed.

Nonetheless, the election results showed Keighley Liberals still in control, for the time being at least: S. O. Buckmaster (Liberal) 4,667; W. M. Acworth (Conservative and Unionist) 3,842; W. C. Anderson (Labour) 3,452.

Activity outside a brand-new Carnegie Free Library during the summer of 1904 as lines are laid for electric trams. Keighley Corporation Tramways had discontinued its horse-drawn service that May, and would open an electrified system in October.

As can be deduced from the triangular track layout, this point at the top of Cavendish Street was to be the centre of a system which would operate routes to Ingrow, Utley and Stockbridge.

In contrast to their rather homely predecessors, the new electric trams would sport a smart white and crimson livery and would carry 3,589 passengers on their first day.

The Oxenhope Industrial and Provident Society Limited prepares to trundle a meticulous display of Co-operative Corn Flour and C.W.S. Marmalade through the village at the start of a gala procession in Leeming.

By the early years of the century, the Co-operative movement had diversified into most aspects of life. The Lees and Cross Roads Co-operative Industrial Society Limited not only operated grocery, drapery, butchering and boot and clog departments, but also delivered coal, ran a savings bank and, from 1905, organised an annual Children's Festival.

The Keighley Industrial Co-operative Society Limited, in addition to a comprehensive range of departments and some manufactures, built houses, ran a restaurant, and offered its members such amenities as a library and newsroom, educational lectures and ambulance classes, and published a periodical, the *Keighley Co-operative Bee*. By 1910 the Keighley Society had a Central Store plus twenty-four branches, employing 283.

Seven of the 24 staff of the Keighley Industrial Co-operative Society's Butchering Department line up for the camera outside their Brunswick Street premises. There was also a Co-operative Society abattoir in Parkwood Street.

This Butchering Department demonstrated 'the true Co-operative principle of providing a thoroughly good article, apart from the mere consideration of the profit derivable from it'. The manager regularly attended cattle markets at Leeds, Skipton and Long Preston, even visiting Craven farms to pick suitable beasts.

During a twelve-month period from July, 1909, to June, 1910, the Butchering Department dealt with 978 cattle (total weight 37,613 stones), 3,128 sheep and 1,351 pigs.

Horse and cattle fairs were traditional highlights in the calendars of many communities. This is the Junction sheep fair held at Cross Hills each autumn. In September, 1908, this drew 'a good number of sheep' and 'a fair attendance of buyers'. There were similar comments in 1909, though trade was slack. Other autumn sheep fairs were held nearby at Malsis and Silsden, whilst at Oxenhope a cattle fair still occupied ground adjoining the Bay Horse Inn at Uppertown.

Meanwhile in Keighley, increasing traffic, and more specifically the tramlines, had pushed the twice-yearly horse and cattle fairs off the main roads into side streets. Cows stood in Scott Street, Russell Street and Devonshire Street, horses at the bottom of West Lane and in the playground of the National School, and sheep round the back of High Street. Afterwards, the Fire Brigade would hose everywhere down!

Notwithstanding 'the unsatisfactory arrangements made for holding these fairs', the Keighley spring fair of 1910 drew a good attendance and brisk business, with prime beasts commanding high prices — a milking cow cost from £15 to £21. That year, too, some 150 horses came to the Keighley fair. Many were heavy cart-horses fetching between £25 and £40.

This photograph shows a cattle fair in Devonshire Street. The prominent building on the right is the Devonshire Street Congregational Chapel, regarded as a smart place of worship attended on Sunday mornings by several families with carriages. It is said that the coachmen, who would sit on the back row, would respectfully go out during the singing of the last hymn in order to bring the carriages to the front door.

The Keighley Union Infirmary up Fell Lane was extended at the turn of the century, with new convalescent, infirm and female imbecile blocks and steam cooking apparatus. These are the two phthisis pavillions erected in 1904 for the accommodation of consumptives.

Administered by the Keighley Board of Guardians in conjunction with the Workhouse, the Infirmary took in some interesting patients. Here in 1899 died 'John' — full name John Dodgson — a familiar figure with his concertina, who had 'rendered appreciated service to the inmates of the Workhouse and Infirmary by going about the wards at Christmas and other times and playing selections'.

'Old Sergeant' Thomas Callaghan died at the Infirmary in 1904. A veteran of the Royal Marine Artillery, he had served in the trenches before Sebastopol during the Crimean War, also in the Indian Mutiny and the Chinese War. He had pawned his medals and had spent the last ten of his 74 years in the Workhouse.

THE MAGGOTORIUM

This Edwardian postcard entitled the Maggotorium commemorates an attempted 'cure for the terrible scourge of consumption'.

At Erlings Quarry, between Denholme and Thornton in the years before the Great War, Messrs A. Bryant and Co. slaughtered horses, boiled bones, and bred maggots. The resulting gases — or effluvia, as they were termed in the trade — were considered beneficial to consumptives, and Messrs Bryant and Co. conceived the notion of inviting sufferers on to their premises. By 1911, 'patients' at the maggot-farm were described as 'inhaling the gases given off by sitting in the same room and at the side of the troughs in which the maggots are actually breeding'. They helped pass the time by reading or playing cards.

There was even an export trade in 'sawdust impregnated with' the precious effluvia; a thousand boxes a week were said to go to hospitals and sanatoria all over the country, even to Toronto!

In 1911 Messrs Bryant and Co. commissioned plans for 'a sanatorium of galvanised iron, giving 150 feet floor space, and 1,500 cubic feet air space for each patient, and with through ventilation'. By way of environmental bonus, outside nuisance ('if any at present exists') would be minimised 'because of the gases being inhaled by the patients instead of being diffused in the atmosphere'.

Despite Bryants' desire to 'do some little good to humanity', their ambitious project does not seem to have come to fruition, and their Maggotorium remained the homely establishment seen in the photograph.

This debonair gentleman leaning on a classical nude statue outside Highfield House was one of the pillars of Edwardian Keighley. Dr William Scatterty, Medical Officer of Health from 1892 to 1928, was also doyen of the Keighley St John Ambulance Brigade, and during the Great War was to serve as Administrator of the Keighley War Hospital, rising to the rank of Lieutenant-Colonel in the Royal Army Medical Corps.

His statue prompted an anonymous postcard addressed to his wife in 1909:

"Dear Mrs Scatterty,
    Please excuse my calling your attention to the Female Figure in the corner of your garden. I been a Female like yourself think it very unbecoming, moreover the Gentlemen are making remarks as they pass, only the other day School Boys were calling for the School Girls to come and look at yourselves. If your Husband take delight in such, well he might have it placed where the public cannot see it. Its indecent.   Yours,
                                              A passer daily."

Dr Scatterty's response seems to have been to have himself photographed with his statue. Presumably the black figure sheltering from the sun on the left is intended to suggest the reality of the female form divine in 1909!

Lads' hobbies of the period often revolved round a hutch or a pen. Here are Herbert and Arthur Jarman with their prize-winning guinea-pigs.

Herbert's career as an exhibitor seems to have begun at the Keighley Agricultural Show in 1909, when he was listed in fourth place in the rabbits section for 'any variety (local), never having won a first prize in open competition to date of entry, buck or doe'. He also came second for 'any variety (except Dutch), prize not to exceed 10s., buck or doe'.

Young Arthur Jarman was to die of smallpox at Basra during the Great War.

When the Jarman brothers commemorated this particular success they went, not to a fashionable portrait studio, but to Amos Dewhirst, the local newsagent and stationer, who contrived this appealing effect with one cup, two boys, three guinea-pigs and a box on a table!

Music was another enthusiastic interest. This photograph by Amos Dewhirst shows his son Elvey (named after Sir George Elvey, a Victorian composer of hymns and oratorios), who became proficient on drums and xylophone, playing in his teens with his father's Orchestral Band and the Keighley and District Orchestral Society. Elvey Dewhirst would die, aged 23, after a motorcycle accident whilst rehearsing for the part of Frederic in an amateur production of Gilbert and Sullivan's 'The Pirates of Penzance'.

In an area notable for its brass bands, Silsden's looked distinctive by virtue of its white tunics. This uniform commemorated its close Victorian links with the Lancashire Militia; indeed, Silsden bandsmen had gone out to the Ionian Islands with the Lancashire Militia band during the Crimean War.

Silsden Brass Band had also had a famous member in Edward Newton, musician, conductor, adjudicator, instructor, arranger and composer of nearly a thousand tunes — anthems, hymns, songs, marches, polkas, fantasias... When Silsden had won third prize at the Belle Vue contest of 1863, it had played a piece arranged by Edward Newton.

This photograph dates from about 1909. So well-known was the Silsden Brass Band of this period that, some twenty years ago, a local resident was still able to supply every name. Viz. left to right:

Back row: E. Clarkson, R. Clarkson, F. Tillotson, F. Dixon, R. Bradley, G. Tillotson.
Middle row: J. Vickers (conductor), J. Taylor, S. Holgate, W. Taylor, E. Booth, J. Clarkson, S. Fortune, G. Laycock.
Front row: E. Verity, J. Baldwin, T. Green, A. Townson, J. Fortune, M. Spencer.

Out of deference to a craze of the time, the Keighley Gala Committee in 1901 instituted a comic band contest, whose entrants marched in the procession and were then judged on stage. The comic band was a development from the earlier bletherhead or bladder-head bands. Bandsmen, according to contemporary account, 'were provided with all manner of 'instruments', and were decked out in all sorts, shapes and shades of costume.' Despite the exotic appearance of their home-made instruments, a staple feature was the kazoo or tommy-talker — a little tin toy blown to produce a raucous noise.

The Keighley Wiffum Waffum Wuffum Band, complete with hobby-horse, won first prize for four years in succession, from 1902 to 1905. They recruited their members from the Eastwood Conservative and Unionist Club in Dalton Lane. Their rendition of an extravaganza called 'The Death of Nelson' would end with everybody laid flat on the ground in the shape of a star! In Gala processions, the Wiffum Waffum Wuffum are said to have always performed 'The Death of Nelson' at the top of Eastwood Row, where many of the bandsmen lived.

Comic bands vied with one another in the outlandishness of their titles. The Haworth Bingem Bangem Band enjoyed a three-year run of taking second prize, against such opposition as Otley Splishem Splashem Splushum, Bradford City Ragtag and the Skipton Belle Vue Doffers.

Nothing better epitomises the palmy flavour of this garden party at 'Wildfell', Oakworth, than the description written on the back of the original print:

'Left to right: Mrs Hanson, Mrs Newsholme, Miss S Cockshott (Governor of Keighley Girls' Grammar School), Mr Hanson, Miss Patty Cockshott (seated), Mrs Bettison (Colonel Sugden's sister), Lady Haggas (The Manor), Mrs Bettison's companion, Colonel Sugden.' The writer didn't bother to identify the children!

'Wildfell' was the home of the Misses Cockshott; Lady Haggas the wife of Sir James Haggas, of Ingrow Mills.

Colonel John Sugden, of 'Hamworth', Oakworth, was the last active family member of Messrs Jonas Sugden and Brothers of Vale Mill. A staunch Liberal, member successively of the Oakworth Local Board and Disrict Council, he retained his military rank as an honorary memento of his involvement in the Volunteer movement and his former command of the 6th Duke of Wellington's West Riding Regiment.

The gentleman on the right of this group is the famous Kirkcudbright artist, Edward Atkinson Hornel, now best remembered for his paintings of girls posed against coastal panoramas. His sister is seated in the centre, with the younger daughter of Tom Clifton Butterfield, who stands on the left, next to his wife, with his elder daughter on the right. The photograph was taken outside the Butterfields' home, the substantial 'Airewood' at Thwaites Brow.

Edwardian Thwaites Brow was noteworthy for its cultured residents, a community of teachers, architects and artists. Tom Clifton Butterfield had been appointed headmaster of the Keighley School of Art in 1889, a post he would hold for thirty years until failing eyesight forced his premature retirement.

He was also a gifted watercolour artist, who drew much of his inspiration from the local landscape. 'November 30, 1912,' he pencilled on the back of a wintry view in nearby Park Wood. 'Keen frost froze the paint as fast as put on.' He exhibited as far afield as the Glasgow Institute of Fine Arts, and when in 1900 Andrew Carnegie was presented with the Freedom of Keighley Borough, it was Mr Butterfield who illuminated his address.

His daughter Dorothy — the young girl seen here on Miss Hornel's knee — would also become a teacher at the Keighley School of Art, and her work was chosen for a touring exhibition in Australia.

This watercolour painted by Tom Clifton Butterfield in 1913 conveys the beauty and comparative tranquillity of Airedale in a slower era, when sheaves were still bound by hand at harvest-time. We are looking from Utley towards Steeton, with the Jubilee Tower of 1887 prominent on the skyline to the left.

GLEN BRIDGE
NR KEIGHLEY

Days out could seem very modest by modern standards. Popular local beauty spots abounded, such as Newsholme Dean, Heather Glen, Goit Stock and Sunnydale. At Glen Bridge, near Laycock, the attractions — other than those provided by Nature — consisted simply of seats, swings and a cottage selling refreshments.

Simple pleasures in an unidentified recreation ground on what could be a chilly Easter. One popular Bank Holiday ritual was walking over Ilkley Moor. On the eve of the Great War, a young servant-girl expressed her obvious delight in such a treat in a letter to her mother:

'We walked away all on the moors and never saw a soul but the Sheep. The west wind was blowing against us all the way & it was lovely. It nearly took our breath at times. We had a lovely view we could see Octley, Menston & the Asylaum Octley Shiven & Arncliffe Craggs' — she meant Almscliffe — 'Guisely Midleton House & the river Warffe & we came to some lovely little streams & ferns growing, & the Heather smelt beautiful & am sending you just a bit.'

The flying-machine has obviously been faked into this photograph as a joke! Otherwise we see a dashing group of young bloods from Ingrow on a waggonette outing.

Horse-drawn waggonettes were commonly used for Edwardian excursions, Bolton Woods being a popular destination. In 1902 the Keighley Glee Union resolved that each member 'be invited to take his wife or sweetheart on the occasion of our trip to Bolton Woods and Skipton'. All must not have gone well, however, as the following year they decided 'that annual excursion be made without wives'!

When the Knowle Park Congregational Mission choir had a waggonette trip to Hardcastle Crags, they 'sung at various places hymns and part songs', but got caught in a thunderstorm on their way home.

This snapshot, on the back of which its amateur photographer scribbled 'At drill, 1902', shows children exercising in the playground at Stanbury Board School.

The photographer — who took hundreds of small views, most of which have faded — was Jonas Bradley, headmaster of Stanbury Board School from 1890 to 1920. He was a prominent local figure, a lantern-lecturer, early member of the Brontë Society, Freemason, President of the Haworth Ramblers, and above all, pioneer of Nature study in schools.

Jonas Bradley believed in taking his scholars outdoors. 'Every Friday afternoon when it is suitable weather,' one little girl wrote in 1906, 'we go out for rambles into the fields. We take with us boxes and lenses, also a note book.' Stanbury schoolchildren were encouraged to undertake such projects as compiling a birds'-nest map of the parish and sending exhibits to a Nature Study Exhibition at Regent's Park. In 1901 a *Yorkshire Post* sub-editor was impressed by their 'newly-hatched tadpoles, insect larvae, pond-snails, water weeds, fossils, flowers of alder, hazel, snowdrop, cleat, & c.'.

'It was the immediate neighbourhood of Stanbury School that offered us the greatest wonders of the world,' recalled a former pupil, many years later, 'and it was Mr Bradley who opened our eyes and taught us to listen.'

These boys and girls from the Haworth Central Board Schools performed maypole dances during Haworth's first annual Demonstration and Gala in the West Lane football field in early June, 1899. Promoted by local friendly societies and the Tradesmen's Association, this raised more than £120 towards the funds of the Haworth and Oxenhope District Nurses' Association formed in 1897.

Such innocent exhibitions were not universally approved of at a time when the Haworth School Board had recently censured the head of the Horkingstone Evening School for teaching dancing. At least one member of the School Board prided himself on being 'a conscientious objector to dancing', but fortunately the Chairman recognised that 'there was all the difference in the world between allowing dancing for young men and women and granting maypole dancing for children', and commonsense prevailed.

Haworth schoolchildren also contributed a May Queen and a demonstration of dumb-bell exercises to the 1899 Gala. This is the May Queen, eleven-year-old Rose Murgatroyd, with her maids of honour. They rode to the field in a waggon, but, as the *Keighley Herald* observed, 'so prettily was it embowered in fresh spring foliage, and decorated with gaily-coloured ribbons, that the unambitious character of the vehicle was not at once apparent'.

In the background is the balloon, the 'Lord Masham', in which Reuben Bramhall of Bradford later made an ascent, accompanied by Charles Merrall of Haworth. They came down near Yeadon.

Balloon ascents provided a popular spectacle on special occasions. Here is Captain Frederick Bidmead, a Londoner with twenty years' ballooning experience, ascending in the 'Falcon' from Victoria Park at the Keighley Hospital Gala in 1908.

He should have gone up on a Saturday evening, but so many people were queueing for a 'journey into cloudland' in the captive balloon — at half-a-crown for three minutes — that his ascent was postponed till the Monday. Several thousands watched. The balloon remained visible from Victoria Park for about forty minutes, descending near Shipley Glen.

Captain Bidmead had hoped to take up two local passengers, but the 'Falcon' proved inadequate for both. Accordingly they tossed a coin, and William Coleman of Thwaites Brow was the lucky one.

Captain Bidmead was well-known in the Keighley district. At the Gala of 1898, his parachute descent from a balloon had gone wrong, leaving him hanging by his fingers some 3,000 feet up. He had survived this predicament for fifty minutes and come down on the farther side of Pontefract! In 1906 his employee, 21-year-old Miss Lily Cove, had been killed whilst making a parachute descent at the Haworth Gala.

TRACTOR BIPLANE AT MANNYWELLS HEIGHTS. PILOT. CAPT. MACLEAN. OCT. 13. 1913.

There was an unexpected sensation in the Denholme and Cullingworth district on Friday, October 10th, 1913, when an Army aeroplane, on a flight from Aldershot to Montrose, came casually down in a field at Manywells Heights, having run short of petrol. Pilot was Captain Maclean of the 1st Scots; the machine a tractor biplane with a 75 horse-power engine.

Petrol was obligingly rushed up by car from a Keighley motor engineers, but the weather meanwhile deteriorated and Maclean decided to stay the night. By first light next morning, hundreds of sightseers were converging on the scene — some of whom managed to scrawl their signatures on the wings and body of the phenomenon! Since the sky remained clouded, the Captain, centre of a hero-worship, delayed his take-off again.

A quaint War Office regulation of the period forbade Army machines from flying on Sundays, so, while its pilot wined and dined in the neighbourhood, the biplane spent the weekend roped off in a corner, its propellor-blades swathed in linen bags. The farmer owning the field made a tidy sum by charging admission.

At last, as seen here on Monday, October 13th, in view of an admiring crowd, Captain Maclean bounced up and away over Harden and Bingley to resume his leisurely flight to Montrose.

Equal first prize for the best decorated house front along the procession route at the Keighley Friendly Societies' Gala of 1903 was won by this pair of next-door neighbours in Victoria Road. Actually, the households were related — the wives of James Wright at No. 17, and of William Lloyd at No. 19, were twin sisters.

The flags and crowns in their joint display suggest that they might have been left over from the previous year's Coronation, but the most impressive effect was achieved by candle-lit lanterns. These were lit when darkness fell, to the admiration of the neighbourhood.

Silsden's first annual Charity Carnival in September of 1908 included a competition for the best decorated shop along the route of its procession. First prize went to greengrocer Emma Throup for this painstaking display in Kirkgate. She has hung what looks like her winner's certificate in the middle of the window.

PROCLAMATION of KING GEORGE the V at HAWORTH MAY 20th 1910

The Chairman of the Haworth District Council, J. Ackroyd, reads the Proclamation of King George V from the steps of the Parish Church on May 20th, 1910.

This ceremony followed a memorial service at Haworth Church. Organisations which had officially attended can be distinguished in the crowd: Haworth Brass Band, the Haworth Detachments of the 6th Battalion of the West Riding Regiment of Territorials and of the Keighley Corps of the St John Ambulance Brigade, the Church Lads' Brigade and the Pewit Patrol of Boy Scouts. Also present are members of the Haworth District Council, the police force, the fire brigade and friendly societies.

Ian Dewhirst was born at Keighley in 1936 and was educated at Keighley Boys' Grammar School and the University of Manchester. After National Service as a Sergeant-Instructor in the Royal Army Educational Corps, he started work in 1960 at Keighley Public Library, where he was Reference Librarian from 1967 until taking early retirement in 1991. He writes and lectures extensively on local history, and is the compiler of three collections by Hendon Publishing Company, *Old Keighley in Photographs*, *More Old Keighley in Photographs* and *Keighley in the 1930s and '40s*. His other books include *Gleanings from Victorian Yorkshire* (Ridings Publishing Company, 1972), *Gleanings from Edwardian Yorkshire* (Ridings Publishing Company, 1975), *A History of Keighley* (Keighley Corporation, 1974), *Yorkshire Through the Years* (Batsford, 1975), *The Story of a Nobody* (Mills and Boon, 1980), *You Don't Remember Bananas* (Ridings Publishing Company, 1985), *Keighley in Old Picture Postcards* (European Library, 1987), and *Victorian Keighley Characters* (Hendon Publishing Company, 1990).

Holme House
Wood,
Keighley

THE LOVERS Walk

Cynicus

Photographs showing Edwardian courting couples are hard to find, but this postcard by 'Cynicus' — allowing for artistic licence! — illustrates the popularity of Holme House Wood as a 'Lovers' Walk'. Actually, the postcard enjoyed a country-wide circulation, as the names of local courting venues could be printed separately on to the basic design.

404

Office staff at work, probably in one of the larger Keighley textile concerns. Although the scene bristles with possible clues — at least three business calendars and two shelves of labelled box-files — none are quite decipherable, and the only distinguishable fact is that it is ten past ten in the morning! Note the office-boy towards the right in his stiff white collar, and the men standing at their desks.